Use felt board props w/ this book

BIBLE STORIES
for little children

VOLUME ONE, Revised Edition

by Betty R. Hollender

illustrated by Lee Bearson

UNION OF AMERICAN HEBREW CONGREGATIONS
New York, New York

TO HERBERT

Library of Congress Cataloging-in-Publication Data

Hollender, Betty R.
  Bible stories for little children.

  Summary: An illustrated retelling of the stories found
in the Old Testament.
  1. Bible stories, English—O.T. [1. Bible stories—
O.T.] I. Bearson, Lee, ill. II. Title.
BS551.2.H6 1985   221.9'505   85-24708

Publication of this book was made possible
by a generous bequest from the estate of
GERTRUDE COHN GREENBERG

May her memory be for a blessing

Introduction

Stories from the Bible are a rich source of Jewish literacy and identity. No wonder, then, that Jews of all ages tell and retell stories of the matriarchs, patriarchs, kings, and prophets.

Children love stories. And what better gift can we give to our sons and daughters than the treasure of Torah, made accessible to them at precisely the moment they begin to read. In bringing biblical characters to life, in presenting them with all their strengths and all their shortcomings, in emphasizing the values that their lives embodied, we say to our children: You, too, can be a Jewish leader. You, too, can make a difference.

For some three decades, Betty Hollender's *Bible Stories for Little Children* has been read and enjoyed by hundreds of thousands of young people. Now recast in a more contemporary style, Ms. Hollender's stories will enable the study of Torah for yet another generation.

We are proud to bring this special volume to you, and we hope that it will be widely used in both classrooms and homes throughout North America.

Rabbi Daniel B. Syme

Thank You

I would like to thank the many people who prepared this book for publication. I wish to thank particularly Rabbi Daniel B. Syme, Rabbi Howard I. Bogot, Stuart L. Benick, Aron Hirt-Manheimer, Annette Abramson, Josette Knight, and the artist Lee Bearson whose delightful pictures interpret the spirit of the text so well.

Thanks in addition to my husband Herbert for his enthusiasm and support in this and all my creative efforts.

Betty R. Hollender

CONTENTS

NOAH'S ARK

Did you ever see an ark?
An ark looks like a houseboat.
The first ark had animals living in it.
Listen and I will tell you about the first ark.

Once upon a time, according to a story in our Torah,
a good man named Noah had a big adventure.

One day, God sent Noah a message.
"Noah, Noah. A flood is coming.
Rain is coming.
The rain will come down, down, down.
It will cover the trees.
The rain will come down, down, down.
It will cover the mountains, too.

"Noah, Noah, make an ark.
Save your family from the flood.
Make an ark to float on the waters.
Take two of every kind of animal with you.

"Take two lions, take two monkeys,
Take two turtles, and two donkeys.
Take two pandas, kangaroos,
Take two elephants, two gnus.
Take two crocodiles lying in the sun,
Take two lizards when their nap is done.
Take giraffes with necks so tall,
Tigers, zebras, take them all.

Take big, black rhinoceroses,
Two big hippopotamuses,
Two big, sprawling octopuses—
Take them, take them, take them all.
Take the flies and take the bees,
All the insects your eye sees.
Take two robins, eagles, too,
Hawks and bluejays take with you.
Take two sea gulls, take two doves—
Flying high, high above.
Save them from the flood, too."

So Noah made the ark.
Shem, Ham, and Japheth, his sons, helped him.
Noah cut down the trees.
"Shem," he said, "saw the tree trunks into boards.
Ham, you are a good worker; nail the boards together.
Japheth, you can melt some tar so no water can get
inside the ark."

"Father," said Japheth, "Father, the tar is bubbly.
Is it ready, Father? Is it ready?"

"Yes," said Noah, "it is ready.
Come, my sons, help me paint the ark with tar.
Help me waterproof it."

Soon Noah said, "This ark is ready for the animals.
We must get two of every kind of animal for our ark.

"Get two lions, get two monkeys,
Get two turtles, and two donkeys.
Get two pandas, kangaroos,
Get two elephants, two gnus.
Get two crocodiles lying in the sun,
Get two lizards when their nap is done.
Get giraffes with necks so tall,
Tigers, zebras, get them all.
Get big, black rhinoceroses,
Two big hippopotamuses,
Two big, sprawling octopuses—
Get them, get them, get them all.
Get the flies and get the bees,
All the insects your eye sees.
Get two robins, eagles, too,
Hawks and bluejays take with you.
Get two sea gulls, get two doves—
Flying high, high above.

"Ham, you may get the animals that run on four feet.
Japheth, you may get the birds.
Be quick!
The rain will come soon."

Noah's sons got the animals.
Noah put them in the ark.
He shut the door.
Then the thunder thundered.
And the lightning was fright'ning.
The rains came.
They came down, down, down.

Pour…pour…pour…
Splash…splash…splash…
Over the ark.

The rains came down and down.
The ark floated away.
The water came up over the trees.
It came up over the mountains.
The ark sailed on the water over the mountains.

It rained for forty days and forty nights.
Then the rain stopped.
"Look," said Ham, "the rain has stopped."

"So it has," said Noah, "so it has.
We will let this little dove fly away.
Maybe it will find some dry land."

So they let the dove fly away.
It came back that night.
It was very tired.
It did not find land.

Noah waited. He waited one day.
He waited two days.
He waited for seven days.
Then Noah let the dove out again.
That night, it came back with an olive branch
in its mouth.
"Good," said Noah, "the water is lower now.
Soon we shall find dry land."

Again Noah waited. He waited one day.
He waited two days.
He waited for seven days.
Then Noah let the dove fly away again.
That night, it did not come back.

"Fine," said Noah, "it has found dry land.
And we shall find some, too."

"Dry land!" shouted Noah.
He anchored the ark.
Noah's sons jumped out onto dry land.
Noah jumped out, too.

They thanked God for keeping them safe
through the great flood.
"God gives us life,
God keeps us safe,
God lets us see this beautiful day.
Thank you, God," they said.

"Look! Look!" shouted Noah.
"Look at the sky!"
Noah's family looked up.
They saw a beautiful rainbow.
"The rainbow is God's message," said Noah.
"It will remind us to work every day to make the earth
clean and green and beautiful."

Everytime we see a rainbow, we remember the story of
Noah and the first rainbow. We look at the rainbow and
say:

> *Baruch Atah Adonai Elohenu Melech
> ha'olam shehecheyanu vekiyemanu
> vehigianu lazeman hazeh.*

> Blessed is the Lord our God, Ruler of the
> universe, for giving us life, for sustaining us,
> and for enabling us to celebrate this festive day.

THE TOWER OF BABEL

Once upon a time, all the people could understand
each other.
They did not have to learn different languages.
Everyone spoke one language.
Everyone was happy until a person asked,
"What is above the sky?"

Everyone answered, "Only God knows.
Well, why shouldn't we know, too!

"Let us build a tower up to the sky.
Then we can see what is above it.
Then we will know what God knows."

"Good, good, good," cheered the people.
"Let's begin. Let's begin."

They all began to work on the tower.
They put down a layer of bricks.
They put mortar on top of the bricks,
and more bricks,
and more mortar,
and more bricks,
and more mortar.

Every day the tower grew a little higher.
Higher and higher it grew.
Nearer and nearer to the sky it grew.

The people wanted to be like God.

But, one day, two people began to fight.
This is the way the fight went:
"You have too much mortar."
"I do not."
"You do so."
"I do not."

Then more people began to fight.
"Get out of my way."
"Watch out," they called.
But nobody got out of the way.
Many people fell off the tower.
Many people got hurt.
Everyone kept shouting, "Get out of my way."

Friends became enemies.
People forgot how to talk to each other.
It was a mixed-up time.
There was yelling,
fighting,
and noise.

People wanted to finish the tower.
But there was too much noise.
There was too much shouting.
They could not plan the work.
They could not finish the tower.

They could not find out what was above the sky.
They never found out
all the things God knows.

ABRAHAM BREAKS THE IDOLS

The first Jew was named Abraham.
When Abraham was a little boy, he lived in the city of Ur.
The people of Ur thought there were many gods.
They thought one god sent them rain.
They thought one god sent them sunshine.
They thought another god sent them food.
And they thought another god made sick people well.
They thought many gods ruled the world.
They did not think about *Adonai Echad*, the One God.
They did not talk about *Adonai*.
They thought about many gods instead.

The people of Ur made their gods look like people.
They made dolls and prayed to them
as they would to gods.
They called the dolls idols.

The people of Ur were afraid of their gods.
They were afraid their gods would punish them.
So they were good to the gods.
They gave them presents.
They prayed to them.
They were good to the gods because they wanted
the gods to be good to them.

Wasn't that silly?
Do you think a doll could be good to you?
Do you think a doll could punish you?

Abraham's father made idols.
He made big idols.
He made middle-sized idols.
He made small idols, too.

Abraham liked to play with the idols.
He liked to pretend they were real people.

One day, Abraham's father had to go away.
He said, "Abraham, you are getting to be a big boy.
I have to go away for a little while.
Are you big enough to take care of the idols for me?"

"Oh, yes, Father," said Abraham,
"I am big enough to take care of the idols for you."

"That is good," said Abraham's father.
"Good-by, Abraham.
Remember to take good care of the idols."

Abraham thought a good way to take care of the idols
was to play a game with them.

He ran over to the biggest idol and said,
"Big idol, you are the father."
He ran over to the middle-sized idol and said,
"Middle-sized idol, you are the mother."
Then he said to all the small idols,
"Little idols, you are the children.
You are very naughty children.
You did not obey your father.
So I will have to spank you."

Abraham pretended to spank the little idols.
Crash! One little idol fell down.
Another little idol fell down and was broken.

"Oh! Oh!" thought Abraham.
"What shall I do?"

He thought and thought.
He thought of a plan.
He put a stick in the biggest idol's hand.

Soon his father came in.
"Abraham, Abraham, what has happened to the idols?"
asked his father.

"The big idol had to spank the little idols because they
were naughty," said Abraham.
"Why Abraham," his father said, "what a funny story!

The idols are dolls.
You know dolls cannot talk.
You know dolls cannot move."

"Why Father," Abraham said, "what are you saying?
You think they can send you rain.
You think they can send you sunshine.
You think they can send you food.
You even think they can make sick people well.
How can they do these things if they cannot talk?
How can they do these things if they cannot move?
Why do you pray to them, Father?"

Abraham's father looked at the idols.
They could not talk.
They could not move.
He did not know why he prayed to them.

"They have eyes," thought Abraham's father,
"but they cannot see.
They have ears, but they cannot hear.
They have lips, but they cannot speak.
They have bodies, but they cannot move.
Abraham, I don't know why I pray to idols,
but I need to pray."

"Don't pray to idols," said Abraham.
"There must be a God who created the world.
We cannot see God, but we can pray to God."
Abraham and his father prayed together:

Adonai Elohenu Adonai Echad!
The Lord is our God, the Lord is One!

ABRAHAM SETTLES A QUARREL

Abraham was Lot's uncle.
He lived near his nephew.
Most of the time they were good friends.
But sometimes they quarreled.

Abraham had many sheep.
Lot had many sheep, too.
Abraham needed grass for his sheep to eat.
And Lot needed grass for his sheep to eat.
Sometimes Lot's sheep would nibble
at Abraham's grass.
And sometimes Abraham's sheep would nibble
at Lot's grass.
Then the shepherds of Abraham and the shepherds of
Lot would fight.

One day, Abraham went to look at his sheep.
The shepherds did not hear him coming.
But he heard their angry voices,
and he saw them fighting.
"Get your sheep out of our grass," said Lot's shepherds.
"Get your sheep out of our grass," said Abraham's
shepherds.

Abraham called to his shepherds,
"What is all this noise about?"
"Their sheep are eating up our grass,"
said Abraham's shepherds.
"No, no," said Lot's shepherds, "your sheep are eating
up our grass."

"Come, come," said Abraham, "there is plenty of grass
for all the sheep.
Let us talk to Lot about this.
Go and get him right away."

Soon the shepherds came back with Lot.
"Our shepherds are fighting," said Abraham.
"They are fighting," said Lot, "because your sheep are
eating up my grass.
So my sheep are getting thin."

"Fighting will not make our sheep fat," replied Abraham.
"Look at all this land.
There is plenty of grass.
There is enough grass for your sheep.
There is enough grass for my sheep, too.
We do not have to quarrel.
I have a plan:
We can divide the land.
You can use all the land on one side.
I will use all the land on the other side.
Let us choose."

"I choose that place," said Lot.
He pointed towards a grassy plain.
"Fine," said Abraham.
"I will stay here.
Now we have enough grass for all our sheep to eat.
We will not have to quarrel.
We can live in peace."

ABRAHAM WELCOMES GUESTS

One day, Abraham had visitors.
Three men had come to see him.
They were hungry and thirsty, so Abraham gave them water to drink and food to eat.
The three men were glad to have the water.
They were glad to have the food.
But, most of all, they were glad to sit down and rest.

After they had rested, the men got up to leave.
"Thank you, Abraham," said the first man.
"Thank you, Abraham," said the second man.
"Thank you for the good meal.
Good-by, Abraham," said the third man.
"You have been very kind to us.
Is there anything we can do for you?"

"Thank you for asking," said Abraham, "but I have everything I want.
I have a good wife, Sarah.
I have many sheep.
I am happy here.
But I do want something else.
I want it very much.
I want very much to have a child.
But I am old, and Sarah is old.
We are too old to have a child."

The three men smiled.
"We have something important to tell you," said the first man.
"You will have a baby soon," said the second man.

"Good-by, Abraham," said the third man.
"May God be with you."
And the three men went away.

Abraham was very happy.
He told Sarah what the three men had said.
Sarah was happy, too.

And do you know what happened?
Abraham and Sarah did have a baby, a baby boy.
They called him Isaac.
Isaac is a Hebrew word that means "he will laugh."
Abraham knew that his house would be full of joy and
laughter now that he had a little boy.

REBECCA IS KIND TO A STRANGER

One day, Abraham called his servant Eliezer.
"Eliezer," said Abraham, "I want you to go on a long trip.
I want you to see my nephew, Bethuel.
He will help you find a wife for Isaac."
"Yes," said Eliezer, "I will go."

Eliezer got ready to go.
He took plenty of food.
He took plenty of water.
He took many gifts with him.
He packed everything on his camels' backs.
Eliezer climbed up on one of the camels.
"Good-by," he called.
"Good-by," called Abraham.
"May God be with you."

Eliezer rode away.
He rode and rode.
He rode all that day, and the next day, and the next day
after that.
One late afternoon, he saw the sun going down.
He was tired, and hot, and thirsty, too.
Eliezer saw something green.
"An oasis," he said.
"An oasis would be a good place to get a drink of water."

Eliezer saw a well on the oasis.
A girl was getting water at the well.
Eliezer looked at the girl.
"I am thirsty," he said.
"Will you give me a drink of water?"

"Yes," said the girl.
Eliezer took the water.
"Your camels must be thirsty, too," she said.
"May I give them some water?"
"Thank you," said Eliezer.
"You have been very kind.
Please tell me your name?"
"My name is Rebecca," the girl said.
"I am the daughter of Bethuel."
"Praised be God that I have found you," said Eliezer.

"I am Eliezer, the servant of Abraham,
the uncle of Bethuel."
"My father must meet you.
Let us hurry to my father's house."

"Father, Father," said Rebecca.
"This man is Eliezer, the servant of Abraham."
"Abraham! How wonderful!" said Bethuel.
"We will have much to talk about.
Tell me about my uncle.
But first eat with us. We can see you are hungry.
Rest with us. We can see you are tired."
"Thank you," said Eliezer, "but first I must tell you why I
have come.

"Abraham sent me here to find a woman who could be
a good wife for his son Isaac.
Your daughter Rebecca is kind.
She is pretty, too.
Rebecca would make a good wife for Isaac.
May I take her to meet Abraham and Isaac?"

Bethuel thought and thought.
Then he said, "Abraham's son should make a good
husband for Rebecca.
Let us ask her what she wants to do.
If Rebecca wants to go with you, I will let her go."

Rebecca did want to go.
The next day, Rebecca and Eliezer rode away together.
They rode back to find Abraham and Isaac.
"Isaac will like you very much," said Eliezer.
"You will make him a good wife."

TWINS—JACOB AND ESAU

Isaac and Rebecca wanted a family.
They wanted a baby to love.
They wanted a baby to hug and kiss.

They wanted a baby to take care of.
Isaac and Rebecca were very lucky.

Isaac and Rebecca had twin boys!
Two babies came to them at the same time.

Rebecca gave a name to each.
"I will call one boy Esau.
And I will call the other boy Jacob," she said.

Esau and Jacob were different.
Esau liked to hunt.
Jacob liked to take care of sheep.
Esau grew up to be a hunter.
Jacob grew up to be a shepherd.
Isaac and Rebecca loved their boys.

Esau and Jacob were like many brothers you know.
They wanted to love each other.
But sometimes they would fight.
Then they would forget all about the fight, and they
would be friends again.

ISAAC BLESSES JACOB

Rebecca loved her son Jacob very much.
She helped Jacob get a very special gift from Isaac.

One day, she said to her husband,
"Isaac, my dear, I want Jacob to marry.
I want him to marry a girl from Ur,
the land where I was born.
Many nice girls live there."
"Very well," said Isaac.
"Let Jacob visit your brother Laban.
He lives in Ur.
Send Jacob to me.
I will talk to him about it."

Jacob went to Isaac.
"Here I am, Father," said Jacob.
"My son," said Isaac, "you are grown up now.
You should find a wife.
Find a wife in Ur.
Go to your Uncle Laban.
He will help you."

"All right, Father," said Jacob.
"I will go.
But when shall I leave?"
"Go tomorrow morning," said Isaac.
"Take whatever you need for the trip.
But, before you go, come here.
I want to bless you."

Jacob went over to Isaac.
Isaac blessed him.

He blessed Jacob with these words:
"God bless you and give you the blessing of Abraham."

"Good-by, Father," said Jacob.
"Thank you for your blessing.
It is a very special gift from you to me."

JACOB SAYS GOOD-BY

Rebecca helped Jacob get ready to go.
"See, Jacob," she said, "here is food for you.
And here are some clothes to take with you.
Do you have everything you need?"
"Yes, Mother, I do," said Jacob.
"Do you have enough water to drink?" asked Rebecca.
"It is hard to find water in the desert.
Be sure you have enough."
"Do not worry, Mother," said Jacob.
"Do not worry at all.
I have everything I need.
I have clothes....
I have food....
I have water....
I even have gifts for Uncle Laban."

"You do have everything," said Rebecca.
"You must go now."
"Good-by, Mother," said Jacob.
"Do not worry.
I will be all right."
And Jacob rode away into the desert.

27

THE WONDERFUL LADDER

Jacob was thirsty and sleepy.
He was hungry, and he was very hot.
So he stopped.
He drank some water.
He ate some food.
He lay down and went to sleep.

He had a wonderful sleep.
He dreamed a wonderful dream.
He dreamed he saw a ladder.
The ladder was standing on the ground.
It went up … up … up.
It went way up into the sky.
Jacob could not see the top of the ladder.
It went too high up into the sky.
"What kind of a ladder is this," thought Jacob.
"Where does it end?
What is at the top of the ladder?"

Jacob thought and thought about the ladder.
Soon he believed he heard *Adonai* calling him.
"I am Adonai, the God of Abraham
and the God of Isaac.
I am your God, too.
Do not be afraid, Jacob.
I will always be with you."

Jacob listened and listened,
but *Adonai* did not speak again.
He looked for the ladder, but the ladder was not there.
The sun was shining.
Jacob was wide awake.

"Maybe I had a dream," thought Jacob, "but I know that
Adonai is with me.
He will take care of me always.
I know because I have a special feeling inside of me."

JACOB MEETS RACHEL

Jacob came to Ur.
He saw some shepherds near a well.
"Shalom. Peace be with you," said Jacob.
"Shalom, stranger," answered the shepherds.
"Do you know my Uncle Laban?" asked Jacob.
"Yes, we know Laban," said the shepherds.
"How is my Uncle Laban?" asked Jacob.
"Laban is a proud father," said one of the shepherds.
"Yes, you have a very beautiful cousin,"
said another shepherd.
"Look over there," said a third shepherd.
"Here comes your cousin now."

Jacob looked.
He saw a beautiful girl.
The girl led her sheep to the well.
She wanted to give them water.
The shepherds did not move.
They did not move to help the girl.
But Jacob jumped up.
He went to the well.
A big stone was on top of the well.
Jacob pushed the stone, but the stone did not move.
He pushed harder and harder.
He pushed as hard as he could.
And the stone rolled off the top of the well.

"Come," said Jacob, "I will give some water
to your sheep."
"Thank you, stranger," said Rachel.
"I am no stranger," said Jacob.

"I am your cousin Jacob.
Laban, your father, is my uncle."
"I must run to tell father that you are here."
Rachel ran to find Laban.

"Father, Father," called Rachel.
"Yes, Rachel," answered Laban, "what is the matter?"
"I was taking care of the sheep," said Rachel.
"A man came over to me.
He helped me get water for the sheep.
He says he is your nephew.
He says his name is Jacob."

"Are you sure it was Jacob?" asked Laban.
"I will go at once to greet him.
He must come home and stay with us."
And that is how Jacob came to live with Laban.

THE BROTHERS MEET AGAIN

Jacob and Rachel were very happy.
But Jacob wanted to go back to Canaan.
He wanted to live in the country of his father.
He wanted to take his family to that country.
And he wanted his family to live there.

Jacob wanted to go back to Canaan, but he was afraid.
"Esau, my brother, lives in Canaan," thought Jacob.

"Esau wanted my father's blessing, but father gave it to me.
Will Esau be angry with me?
Will he still be angry because of the blessing?
Maybe he does not remember about the blessing.
Maybe he will say, 'Jacob, my brother, I am happy to see you.'
I must go to Canaan and find Esau.
Maybe Esau is not angry any more."

So, one day, Jacob said, "Rachel!
We are going back to Canaan.
Get ready to go.
Tell your sister Leah to get ready to go.
Tell everyone to get ready to go.
We are all going back to Canaan."

Leah and Rachel got ready to go.
Everyone got ready to go back to Canaan with Jacob.
When everyone was ready, Jacob said,
"Follow me, everyone.
Follow me back to Canaan."

Jacob sent messengers ahead.
He sent them ahead to meet Esau.
"Give Esau these gifts," said Jacob.
"Say to Esau, 'Jacob is our leader.
He wants to meet with you.
Jacob is coming now'."

The messengers found Esau.
They gave him the gifts.
"Jacob is coming to see you," they said.
"He has come from Ur.
He is on his way to Canaan."

"Tell Jacob I will be glad to see him," said Esau.
"Tell him that I am coming to meet him."

So Esau came to meet Jacob.
He looked and looked at his brother Jacob.
Jacob looked and looked at his brother Esau.
They hugged each other.
They kissed each other.
They cried because they were so happy.

A GIFT FOR JOSEPH

Jacob had twelve sons.
He loved them all.
But Joseph was his favorite.
One day, Jacob gave Joseph a coat.
Did it have bright flowers?
Did it have a big picture on the back?
Were there words on Joseph's new coat?
No! No! No!

Joseph's coat did not have flowers.
His gift from his father, Jacob, was not decorated
with pictures or with words.
Joseph's coat was striped.
It was a beautiful, striped coat.

Joseph wore this new coat everywhere.
He wanted his brothers to see it.
He wanted everyone to see it.
He wanted everyone to see how much
his father loved him.
He wanted everyone to say, "Do you see that boy?
Do you see his coat?
His father made him that fancy, striped coat.
He made it because he loved Joseph very much."

JOSEPH DREAMS

Joseph had many dreams.
He liked to talk about them.

He told his dreams to anybody who would listen.
Joseph told his brothers about one dream that made
them very, very angry.
"I saw the sun up in the sky.
I saw the moon up in the sky, too.
And I saw eleven stars up in the sky.
Do you know what they all did?
They all bowed down to me.
They really did.
They all bowed down to me."

Joseph's brothers did not like this dream.
They thought that they were the eleven stars.
They did not want to bow down to Joseph.

Joseph saw that his brothers did not like his dream.
They did not want to hear about Joseph's dreams.
But Joseph liked to talk about himself.
He liked to talk about his dreams.
Joseph kept telling his brothers about dreams in which
he was the most important person.

JOSEPH IS BROUGHT TO EGYPT

Jacob had many sheep.
His sons took care of the sheep.

One day, Joseph brought lunch to his brothers.
Gad saw him coming.
"Look, look," said Gad.
"Here comes Joseph."
"He thinks he is very important," said Simeon.
"He thinks he is too important," said Dan.
"Maybe we could teach him a lesson,"
said another brother.
"A lesson?" said Dan.
"How could we do that?"
"We could hide his beautiful, striped coat," said Gad.
"We could punish him," said another brother.
"We could put him in that pit over there," said Reuben.
"We must not hurt Joseph.
He is our brother.
We can teach him a lesson, but we must not hurt him."

Joseph was very near his brothers now.
"Hello! Hello!" he called.
"Hello, my brothers.
Here I am.
Here I am with food for you."
"That is fine," said Reuben.
"Come here and give us the food."
"Here it is," said Joseph.
"Thank you for the food," said Judah.
"We are glad that you have come."

"Take off your coat," said Gad.
"We want your beautiful, striped coat.
We want a coat just like yours."
"I will not take off my coat," said Joseph.
"I want to wear it."
"Take off your coat," said Dan, "or we will take it off."
And they did.
They took Joseph.
And they put him in the pit.
"What shall we do with Joseph now?" asked one brother.
"I know," said Judah.
"Do you see all those camels?
And do you see the men riding the camels?
Those men are merchants.
Let us talk to them.
Let us see what they are selling.
Maybe they need someone strong to help them."

The brothers went over to the merchants.
They began to talk with them.
"Where are you going?" they asked.
"We are going to Egypt."
"What will you sell there?" asked the brothers.
"We have spices to sell," said the merchants.
"The Egyptians need our spices.
We need their cotton.
They will sell us cotton.
And we will sell them spices."
"You have such a big load," said Asher.
"You need someone to help you."
"We do need someone," said the merchants.
"But the person must be strong."

"We have just the one for you," said Gad.
"Yes.
We have just the right one."
"Where is this person?" asked the merchants.
"Bring that person here for us to see."

The brothers got Joseph.
They showed him to the merchants.
"Hmmm," said the merchants.
"He does look strong.
We will take him with us."
And that is how Joseph was taken from his home.

JOSEPH IN JAIL

The traders came to Egypt.
They sold their spices in Egypt.
They filled their wagons with beautiful cotton.
They sold Joseph, too.
They sold him to a rich man named Potiphar.
And that is how Joseph came to Egypt.

Joseph was happy in Potiphar's house.
But Potiphar's wife was not happy with Joseph.
She did not like him.
"I will get Joseph out of this house," she said to herself.
"I will tell Potiphar that Joseph is not doing his work.
I will make up some stories about Joseph.
Potiphar will be angry at Joseph.
He will put Joseph in jail."
And that is what happened.
Potiphar believed his wife's stories.
And he put Joseph in jail.

The guard in the jail liked Joseph very much.
He let Joseph help feed the other prisoners.

One day, two new prisoners came to the jail.
The king of Egypt who was called the Pharaoh
sent them there.

They were his cupbearer and his baker.
One night, the cupbearer dreamed a dream.
That same night, the baker dreamed a dream, too.

In the morning, Joseph brought them breakfast.
"What is the matter?" asked Joseph.

"You do not look happy, cupbearer.
And you, baker, do not look happy either."

The cupbearer said, "I dreamed a dream.
The baker did, too.
The dreams frightened us, and we don't know
what to do."
"Oh," laughed Joseph.
"Do not be unhappy.
I can tell you what the dreams mean.
Let the cupbearer tell his dream first."

"I dreamed I saw a plant," said the cupbearer.
"It had three branches.
The branches had buds.
The buds turned into flowers.
The flowers turned into grapes.

I pressed the grapes into the king's cup.
They made good wine for the king.
He drank it all up."

"Do not be unhappy," said Joseph.
"Your dream means that Pharaoh
will call you back soon.
He wants you to be his cupbearer again."

"What about my dream?" asked the baker.
"What about my dream?"
"Tell me your dream," said Joseph.

"I had three baskets of bread on my head,"
said the baker.
"Some birds saw the bread.
The bread was for the king.
But the birds wanted it.
They ate it all up.
And there was no bread left for the king."
"Is that all of your dream?" asked Joseph.
"Yes," answered the baker.
"That is all of my dream."
"The king is still angry with you," said Joseph.
"He does not want you to be his baker any longer."
"That cannot be right," said the baker.
"No, no.
That cannot be right."

But it was right.
The king called the cupbearer to return
to the royal palace.
He did not call the baker.

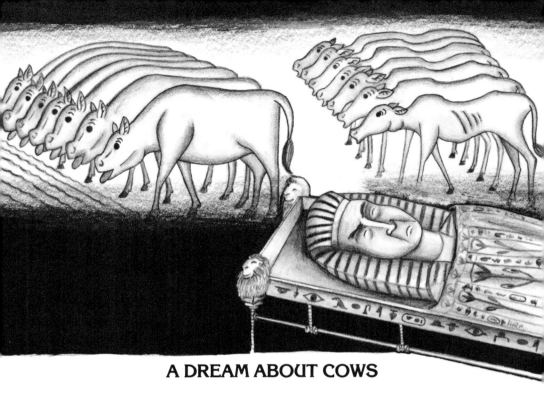

A DREAM ABOUT COWS

One night, the Pharaoh had a bad dream.
He woke up frightened.
"Wise men. Wise men," he shouted.
"Come! Tell me!
What does my dream mean?"

The wise men came.
"What is your dream?" asked the first wise man.
"Tell us your dream," said the second wise man.
"Let us hear your dream," said the third wise man.

"This is my dream," said the Pharaoh.
"Seven fat cows were eating grass by the side
of the river.
Then seven very thin cows joined them.
The seven thin cows were hungry.
They were so hungry that they ate up the seven fat cows.

"Seven thin cows ate seven fat cows, but the thin cows
were still thin, and they were still hungry.
And they did not look one bit fatter."

"What a queer dream.
We do not know what it means,"
said the three wise men.
"What kind of wise men are you?" shouted Pharaoh.
"You cannot even tell what a dream means.
Go away.
I will find someone who can."

The cupbearer heard the king shouting.
He remembered Joseph.
"My lord," said the cupbearer, "I cannot tell what your
dream means."
"Then go away," said the Pharaoh.
"But I know a man who can.
His name is Joseph.
He is in prison."
"Do not stand there," said the king.
"Go and get Joseph at once."
So the cupbearer went to find Joseph.

He brought Joseph to the Pharaoh.
"Can you tell me what my dream means?"
asked the Pharaoh.
"I will try," said Joseph.
"If God helps me, I will succeed."

"This is my dream," said the Pharaoh.
"Seven fat cows were eating grass.
Seven thin cows were eating grass, too.

The thin cows ate up all the grass.
But they were still hungry.
And they were still thin.
So they ate up all the fat cows.
But they were still hungry.
And they did not look one bit fatter."

Joseph looked at the Pharaoh and said,
"The seven fat cows in your dream mean seven years,
seven years when corn will grow in Egypt.
The seven thin cows mean seven years,
seven years when corn will not grow in Egypt.
For seven years the people will have enough to eat.
But, for the next seven years, no corn will grow.
There will be no food at all.
The people will be hungry.

"How can I make the corn grow?" asked the Pharaoh.
"You cannot make the corn grow," said Joseph.
"Only God can do that.
But you can gather corn in the good years.
You can keep it.
You can store it and have it for the bad years.
Then your people will have enough to eat.
They will not be hungry in the bad years."

"That is a good plan," said the Pharaoh.
"Joseph, you must help me. You must take care
of the plan.
Keep enough corn for the bad years.
See that the people do not go hungry."
And that is just what Joseph did.

JOSEPH STORES GRAIN

Joseph built storehouses for the grain.
He talked to the people.
"You must bring me all the corn you do not eat,"
he said.
"Pharaoh has commanded this.
I will keep the corn in the storehouses till you need it."

The people brought their corn to Joseph.
He stored it in the big storehouses.
He kept it, and kept it, and kept it.
He kept it till the seven years were over.

The next year, the corn did not get yellow and sweet.
It hardly grew at all.
The corn could not be eaten.
The people were hungry.
They did not know what to do.

"Come to me," said Joseph.
"I will give you corn.
You will not be hungry."
So the people came to Joseph.
He gave them corn from the storehouses.
They loved him because he gave them corn.

A TIME OF FAMINE (HUNGER)

People were hungry in Egypt.
People were hungry in Canaan, too.
Joseph's father and brothers lived in Canaan.
They had no food to eat.
And they were very hungry.

One day, Joseph's brother saw a caravan.
A caravan is a parade of camels.
"Look at that caravan," said the brothers.
"Maybe it is carrying corn.
Maybe it has corn to sell.
Let us go and see."

The brothers ran to the caravan.
"Do you have any corn to sell?" asked Gad.
"Our father Jacob is old.
He is very hungry.
We are hungry, too."

"We do not have any corn to sell," said the merchants
who were with the caravan.
"But you can buy corn in Egypt.
Then you will not be hungry.
And your father will not be hungry."

The brothers went home.
"Father, Father!" said Reuben, "we know where
to get corn.
Some merchants said to us,
'There is corn in Egypt.
You can buy it there, and you will not be hungry
anymore'."

"Do not wait any longer," said Jacob.
"Go to Egypt and get the corn.
The other brothers may go with you.
But Benjamin, my youngest son, will stay with me.
Go and get the corn and hurry back."

So the brothers got ready to go.
They took fine gifts.
They took money to buy corn.
They climbed on their donkeys.
"Good-by, Father," they called.
And they rode away over the sand.
They rode away to Egypt.

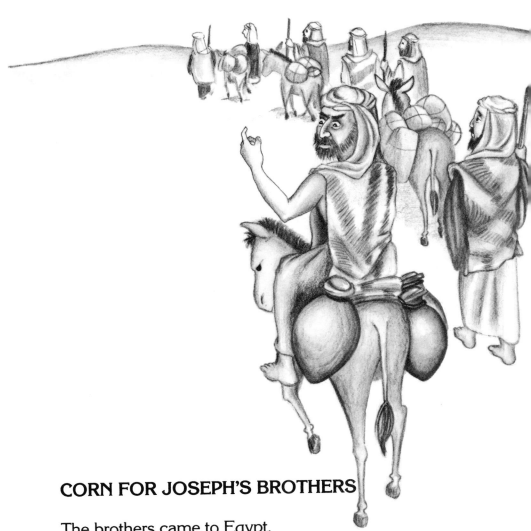

CORN FOR JOSEPH'S BROTHERS

The brothers came to Egypt.
They found the place to buy corn.
They went inside.
Who do you think was there?
Was it the Pharaoh of Egypt?
Was it the cupbearer?
Was it a caravan driver?

No! It was not the Pharaoh.
No! It was not the cupbearer.

No! It was not a caravan driver.
It was Joseph.

Joseph recognized his brothers.
But his brothers did not recognize him.
"I will not tell my brothers who I am," thought Joseph.
"What do you want?" asked Joseph.
"We are hungry," said Judah.
"Our old father is hungry, too.
We have no corn to eat in Canaan.
Will you sell us some?"

"I think you are spies," said Joseph.
"You say that you live in Canaan.
You say that you have an old father.
You say that he is hungry.
But are you telling the truth?"
"We are telling the truth," said Judah.
"We have an old father.
We are twelve brothers.
But one of us has gone away.
And the youngest is at home with our father."

"Bring your youngest brother here," said Joseph.
"Then you may have some corn."
"We cannot bring him here," said Simeon.
"Our father will not let us.
He loves our youngest brother.
He would die if Benjamin did not come back to him."
"Well ...," said Joseph.
"You may have corn this time.
But remember, next time,
bring your youngest brother here."

The brothers took the corn.
They took the corn home to Canaan.
Jacob met them.
"Thank God that you are home again," said Jacob.
"And thank God that you have brought corn.
Now we can make bread.
And we will not be hungry."

Jacob and his sons soon ate up all the corn.
"You must go back to Egypt and get more,"
said Jacob to his sons.
"Benjamin must come with us," said Judah.
"The man said to us, 'Bring your youngest brother or
you will not get any more corn'."

"Benjamin will not go," said Jacob.
"He is my youngest son.
I love Benjamin very much.
If he did not come back to me, I would die.
Once Joseph lived with us.
I loved him very much.
But now he is gone.
I do not have Joseph any more.
I do not want to lose Benjamin, too."

"Oh, Father," said Judah.
"Do not worry about Benjamin.
I will take good care of him."

"We must eat," said Jacob.
"So take Benjamin with you.
But be very careful.
Take good care of him."

THE SILVER CUP

The brothers went to Joseph again.
He asked them many questions.
"How is your old father?
Is he still well?" asked Joseph.
"Where is your youngest brother?
Did you leave him home?"
"Our father is well and happy," said Judah.
"And our brother Benjamin is here with us."

"You shall have your corn," said Joseph.
"I shall have my servants fill your bags.
While the servants fill your bags, you may take
something to eat."
"Thank you," said the brothers.
"We are thirsty, and we are hungry.
We would like something to eat."

So the brothers ate and drank.
Then they climbed on their donkeys.
They rode away into the desert.
They did not ride far.
"Stop! Stop!" a voice called.
The brothers stopped their donkeys.
Joseph's servants had followed them.
They had followed the brothers into the desert.
"What is the matter?" asked Reuben.
The servants answered,
"What is the matter, indeed!
Our master had a silver cup.
He does not have that silver cup now.
You must have it.

How can you be so wicked?
Joseph gives you food to eat,
and you take his silver cup."

"We do not have the cup," said Reuben.
"You may look in our bags of corn.
You will not find the silver cup."
"Yes, yes," said the other brothers.
"Look and see.
Look in our bags of corn.
We do not have the cup."

The servants looked and looked.
They did not find the cup.
They looked in Reuben's bag.
The cup was not there.

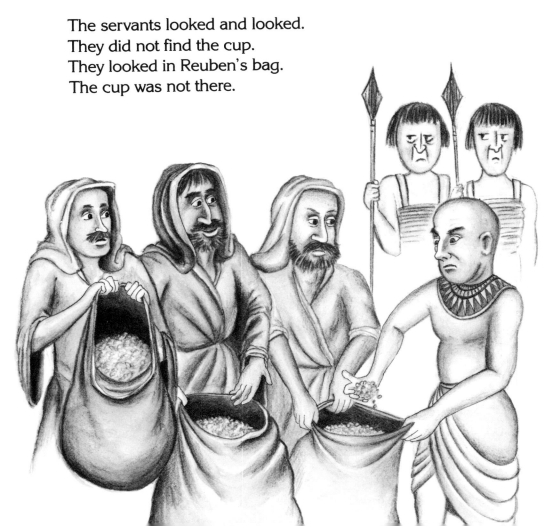

They looked in Simeon's bag.
The cup was not there.
There was no cup in Levi's bag.
There was no cup in Judah's bag.
They opened Dan's bag, but the cup was not there.
They looked in Naphtali's bag; they looked in Gad's bag.
They opened Asher's bag, but they did not find the cup.
They looked in Issachar's bag — no cup.
They looked in Zebulun's bag, but the cup was not there.

There was one more bag to open.
It was Benjamin's bag.
The servants opened Benjamin's bag.
On top of the bag was the *silver cup.*

"That cannot be," said Judah.
"Somebody put that cup into Benjamin's bag.
I know Benjamin did not do it.
Let us go back to speak to your master."

They went back to Joseph.
"We did not take the cup," said Judah.
"Your servants found it in Benjamin's bag,
but we did not take it."

"The boy shall stay with me," said Joseph.
"No," said Judah.
"The boy shall not stay with you.
Our father did not want Benjamin to come to Egypt.
He said, 'I do not have Joseph anymore.
I do not want to lose Benjamin, too'."

Joseph knew that his brothers loved Benjamin.
He knew that they loved their father, too.
He wanted to tell them that he was Joseph.
But he wanted to be alone with them first.
So he said, "Everybody leave this room.
I want to speak to these men alone."

Everybody left the room.
Joseph and his brothers were alone at last.
"Do you not know who I am?" asked Joseph.
The brothers looked at Joseph,
but they did not recognize him.
"I am Joseph.
I am your brother.
Is my father alive?"
"Our father is alive," said Judah.

Now the brothers were afraid.
They had been mean to Joseph.
They had sold him to the merchants.
They were afraid he would be angry with them.
They were afraid he would punish them.

"Come nearer to me," said Joseph.
"Do not be afraid.
I am Joseph, your brother.
You sold me to the merchants.
They took me to Egypt.
And I stayed here.
But do not be afraid.
I am not angry with you.
I am glad to see you.
There is plenty of corn in Egypt.

I can take care of you in Egypt.
And I can take care of Jacob, my father, too.
Take some wagons.
Take some camels.
Go and get my father.
Bring him back here to me.
I have not seen my father in many years."

The brothers went home to Jacob.
"Father, Father," they said, "Joseph is still alive.
He is a leader in Egypt."
"It is enough that my son Joseph is alive.
I will go to see him before I die," said Jacob.

So Jacob and his sons went to Egypt.
They took their wives and children with them.
They took all their belongings and went to Egypt to live.
Judah went ahead.
He showed them the way to go.
When they arrived in Egypt,
Joseph was there to meet them.
He was sitting in his chariot.
He looked like a noble prince.
When he saw his father, he got out of his chariot.
He ran over to his father and kissed him.
"Thank God," said Jacob, "that I have lived to see you.
Thank God that you are alive."

Joseph and Jacob cried because they were so happy
to see each other.
Jacob and his sons came to live with Joseph.
All of Jacob's family moved to Egypt.

A BASKET FOR THE PRINCESS

Many years later, the kind Pharaoh died.
A new Pharaoh ruled over Egypt.
He did not know about Joseph.
He did not know that Joseph had saved
the people of Egypt from famine.

One day, this Pharaoh made a speech.
He said, "All the Hebrews must work for me.
I will not let the Hebrews be free.
From now on, they shall be my slaves."

The Hebrews did not like this.
They did not want to be slaves.
They wanted to be free.
But Pharaoh made them slaves anyway.
He put taskmasters over them.
He made them build his store-cities.
He made them work hard in the hot sun.
The taskmasters hit the Hebrews
to make them work even harder.
Pharaoh was very cruel.
He was so cruel that he even wanted to kill
all the boy babies of the Hebrews.

One of the Hebrew babies was named Moses.
Jochebed was the name of his mother.
Amram was his father.
Moses had a big brother.
His name was Aaron.
Moses had a big sister, too.
Her name was Miriam.

Miriam cried when she heard Pharaoh's plan.
"I want my brother to stay here," said Miriam.
"I want my baby, Moses, to be with us," said Jochebed.
Amram and Aaron wanted to keep Moses, too.
They loved him very much and did not want Pharaoh
to take him away.

They thought they could save the baby.
"Let us make a basket for baby Moses," said his mother.
"We will put the baby in the basket.

We will put the basket by the Nile River.
We will watch it carefully.
Maybe someone will find the baby and be kind to him."

They put the basket by the side of the Nile River.
Miriam's mother went home to wait.
Miriam stayed and hid near the basket.
She watched and watched.
She waited and waited.

Soon Pharaoh's daughter came down to the river
to bathe.
She saw the basket.
She saw the baby in the basket.
"What a beautiful baby," she said.
"I will keep him for my own."
Miriam ran out of her hiding place.
"Please, please," said Miriam, "I know a good nurse.
She is a Hebrew woman.
She can take care of this baby for you.
Please let me get her."

"Certainly," said the princess.
"I will need a good nurse for this baby.
You may go and get her right away."
Soon Miriam came back with her mother.
"Take this baby," said the princess, "and nurse him
for me."
So Miriam and her mother took the baby home again.

This baby grew up to be a very famous man,
our great leader, Moses.

THE BURNING BUSH

Moses grew up in Pharaoh's palace.
He was proud to be a Hebrew.
He saw the Hebrew slaves work hard for Pharaoh.
Moses was sad.
"It isn't fair," thought Moses.
"The Hebrew people should not be slaves.
But what can I do?
Pharaoh will not listen to me."

Moses grew up to be a man.
He was still sad about the slaves.
He left Egypt.
He went to live in the land of Midian.
He lived in the wilderness.
He took care of sheep.
He did not live in the palace any more,
but he did not forget the Hebrew slaves.

One day, Moses was watching his sheep.
A little lamb ran away.
Moses ran after the lamb.
He caught it.
He started back to the other sheep.
Suddenly, Moses stopped.
"This lamb is lucky," thought Moses.
"I saved the lamb.
I always take care of the lambs.
My Hebrew people are not lucky.
They are slaves to Pharaoh.
Who takes care of them?"

Moses felt angry and hot.
The air felt hot; even the ground felt hot.
Everything was so hot that a bush caught fire.
It caught fire, but it did not burn up.

Moses was frightened.
The bush was very frightening.
Moses prayed to *Adonai.*
Then he felt quiet.
He was not angry any more.

"I know who takes care of the Hebrew slaves,"
thought Moses.
"It is *Adonai.*
Adonai can help them if I help *Adonai.*
I must go back to Egypt.
I must tell the slaves, '*Adonai* will set you free.'
I must tell Pharaoh 'Let my people go!'

"But I am afraid.
I cannot speak well.
Pharaoh will never listen to me.
He may listen to Aaron.
Aaron speaks very well.
Aaron will go with me to Pharaoh.
We will tell him, 'Let my people go!'"

LET MY PEOPLE GO!

Moses went to see Pharaoh.
"Let my people go!" he said.
At first, Pharaoh said, "No!
I am Pharaoh, ruler of all Egypt."

"*Adonai* is the ruler of all the world," said Moses.
"*Adonai* wants the Hebrews to be free.
Adonai does not want them to be slaves.
Adonai is stronger than you."

Moses and Aaron went to the Pharaoh ten times.
Each time, Pharaoh said, "I will let your people go.
Tell your God, Moses, I will let them go."
But, each time, the Pharaoh changed his mind.
Ten times Pharaoh promised to let the Hebrews go.
Nine times he changed his mind.

The tenth time, Moses said to the Hebrews,
"Hurry! Hurry! Hurry!
Come as fast as you can."
He said to the men and women,
"Pack everything you need.
Pack everything you need to take out of Egypt.
Bring the food.
Bring all the food you can carry."
He said to the children, "Help your mothers and fathers.
We must leave Egypt now.
Hurry! Hurry! Hurry!"
And the Hebrews did hurry.
The men and women packed everything they needed.
They also brought all the food they could carry.
The children helped.
And the Hebrews hurried to leave Egypt.

They hurried to the Sea of Reeds.
They crossed the Sea of Reeds.
They got across just in time....

Pharaoh changed his mind again.
"The Hebrews must work for me," he said.
"They must build my store-cities.
They must be my slaves."
He called his soldiers.
"Follow the Hebrews," he commanded.
"Bring them back to me."

The soldiers followed the Hebrews.
They used horses and chariots.
Faster and faster went their horses.
Faster and faster went their chariots.
Faster and faster went the soldiers.

But Pharaoh's soldiers were too slow.
The Hebrews had crossed the Sea of Reeds.
They had crossed the Sea of Reeds safely.
But the soldiers could not get across.
And the Hebrews were free at last.

They thanked *Adonai*.
They sang a prayer to God:

>Who is like You, O God, among the mighty?
>Who is like You, glorious in holiness, awe inspiring,
>working wonders? Amen.

THE COMMANDMENTS

Moses led the Hebrew people into the desert.
He led them out of Egypt.
God had set them free.
The people were happy to be free.
But some of the people were not kind to each other.
Some of the people did not tell the truth.
Some of the people were always fighting.
Some of the people took things that belonged to others.

Moses wanted to teach his people how to live together.
But he did not know how to do it.

One day, he said to his people,
"Do you see that mountain?
I must climb it.
I must climb to the very top of the mountain.
I must pray to God for the strength to lead you.
I must help you to become kind and honest.
I must teach you to work for a world of peace.
I must show you how to love each other."

Moses went up to the top of the mountain alone.
At the top, Moses learned about *Adonai*.
He learned that the Hebrew people
must live by God's commandments.
He learned that all people
must live by *Adonai's* commandments.
Moses learned ten commandments
to teach the Hebrew people
when he came down the mountain.
The Hebrew people would teach
these commandments to all people.
Moses wrote the Ten Commandments
on two tablets of stone.

These are some of the commandments:
I am the Lord, your God.
Do not pray to idols.
You must have no other gods but Me.
Remember the Sabbath day to keep it holy.
Honor your father and your mother.
Do not murder.
Do not steal.
Do not tell lies about your friends.
Don't wish for things that belong to other people.

THE GOLDEN CALF

After Moses wrote down the Ten Commandments
on the two stone tablets, he was happy.
He knew the Ten Commandments
would help the Hebrews.
He knew the Ten Commandments
would help them live together happily.

Moses picked up the tablets.
He started to go down, down the mountain.
Down, down the mountain went Moses
with the tablets in his hands.
Soon he came to the bottom of the mountain.
He saw something glittering.
It was glittering in the sun.
He saw the Hebrews dancing around it.
He saw them bowing low before it.
He heard them singing a song to it.
They sang,
"Around, around, around we go!
And as we go, we all bow low.
Around, around, around we go, around the golden calf."

Moses came closer to the Hebrews.
It was true.
The glittering thing was a calf.
It was a golden calf.
The Hebrews were dancing around it.
They were singing to it.
They were bowing low and praying to it.

Moses was very angry.
He could not believe what he heard.
He could not believe what he saw.
He looked again.
The Hebrews were dancing.
They were bowing low.
They were praying to the golden calf.
They were not praying to *Adonai*.

Moses was so angry that he threw the tablets
down to the ground.
Crash! The tablets broke.
The Jews heard the crash.

They came to see what had happened.
Moses told them about the Ten Commandments.
He reminded them about praying to *Adonai*.
They said they were sorry.
They would not pray to an idol again.
They would pray only to *Adonai*.

Moses wanted the Hebrews to have
the Ten Commandments, so he had to go back
to the top of the mountain.
He had to go back up the mountain
and write them all over again.

MOSES BLESSES JOSHUA

Moses was growing old.
He had white hair.
He had a long, white beard.
He walked slowly.
He talked slowly, too.

One day, he called, "Hear, O Israel, come together."

The Hebrews came to hear Moses speak.
"My children," he said, "I am growing old.
I have led you for many years.
But now I need to rest.
You need a new leader, a younger leader.

"Here is the man for you.
His name is Joshua.
Joshua will be your leader now."
"We want you," shouted the Hebrews.
"I am tired.
I need to rest," said Moses.
"You will learn to love Joshua.
He will be a good leader for you.
Come to me, Joshua.
I will bless you."

Joshua came up to Moses.
Moses put his hands on Joshua's head.
And these are the words he used to bless Joshua:

> Be strong and of good courage, for you shall bring
> the Children of Israel into the Promised Land.
> And *Adonai* will be with you. Amen.